How to Study Effectively

Richard Freeman and John Meed

nec
NATIONAL
EXTENSION
COLLEGE

Acknowledgements

How to Study Effectively

© 1972, 1999 National Extension College Trust Ltd.

First published 1972.

Reprinted 1984, 1991.

This revised edition published 1999.

ISBN 1 85356 815 5

Authors: Richard Freeman and John Meed

Revision author: John Meed

Cover design by: Hilary Reed

Page design by: Hilary Reed

Page layout by: Eric Coles

Printed by: Pear Tree Press Ltd

The National Extension College is an educational trust and a registered charity with a distinguished body of Trustees. It is an independent, self-financing organisation. Since it was established in 1963 NEC has pioneered the development of flexible learning for adults. NEC is actively developing innovative materials and systems for open and distance learning opportunities on over 150 courses, from basic skills to degree and professional training.

For further details of NEC resources and supported courses contact:

National Extension College
The Michael Young Centre
Purbeck Road
Cambridge CB2 2HN
Tel: 01223 400200 Fax: 01223 400399

E-mail: info@nec.ac.uk
Homepage: www.nec.ac.uk

Contents

Introduction

Introduction

About the course

How to Study Effectively is an open learning course, designed for students who are learning on their own. It is a fully revised version of one of the most successful open learning courses on study skills. Over 100,000 students have already used *How to Study Effectively*, and their comments include these:

> *After studying the course I felt more confident as it offered very practical advice on each area of study making it much easier than I imagined.*

> *I would like to say how much I have enjoyed the course. I would certainly recommend it as money well spent to anyone returning to learning.*

> *An excellent enjoyable course which has given me confidence and fills me with enthusiasm for further learning.*

> *It has and is continuing to be an exciting time for me.*

The course has now been updated in the light of student and tutor comments, and reflects the latest ideas and research about learning.

Purpose

There is a good chance that you haven't studied recently. You may indeed feel nervous about it. And you probably have many other commitments on your time. You may have a job, a family to look after or other responsibilities.

This course will help you to become a more confident and efficient learner, so that when you are studying you are also learning. In more detail, the course will help you to:

- analyse how you learn most effectively
- identify techniques and resources that will help you learn
- read effectively
- keep useful notes
- write effectively
- prepare for assessment.

Using the course

The course is divided into six units. You should be able to complete a unit in three hours or so, though you may want to spend more time on any units that you find especially helpful. The units contain the following features that will help you learn effectively:

Objectives

Each unit begins with an introduction and objectives. These describe what you will get out of the unit. They give you a clear idea of what you will learn, and you can check with them at the end of the unit to make sure you have understood everything.

Activity

All the units are based on a series of activities. Research into learning shows that people learn better when they are doing something. It is much harder to learn just from reading or listening. So the activities suggest what you should do to achieve the objectives.

Activities may ask you to think about something, to write something down, or to find something out.

Comment

After every activity there is a comment. This gives you feedback on what you may have done, plus extra ideas and suggestions.

Key skill

Note that in a few places you will also see this 'key skill' symbol. This shows points in the course that are relevant to one or more of the key skill units.

ACTION PLAN

At the end of each unit is a summary and action plan which suggests how you can put the ideas in the unit into practice.

A note about using computers

At appropriate points during the course we mention ways in which you could use a computer in your study – in particular wordprocessing and the internet. These suggestions should help the growing number of students who have access to a computer at home, work or in a college. If you do not wish to use a computer you should ignore these references – the course will be just as valuable without one.

How do you learn?

Introduction

You are taking this course because you want to learn as effectively as possible. You may feel that you are not very good at learning at the moment. You may feel that you are out of practice, or rusty. Most people feel this way at some time.

However, this course will show you that learning is a skill – in fact a number of skills – that you can improve and develop. And this unit will show you that in fact you are learning all the time. It will also help you to get to know yourself as a learner, so that you can find out which style of learning suits you best, and to set realistic goals for your study.

Your work on the rest of this course will then be devoted to maximising your own strengths and abilities, and developing the skills you need to succeed.

Objectives

This unit will help you to:

- analyse how you learn

- identify your strengths as a learner

- describe how you feel about studying

- list your reasons for studying

- identify your study goals

- plan your study

- use positive thinking

- identify people who could help you.

How you feel about learning

You may feel that learning is something you only did at school or college, in a classroom, with a teacher. In fact, you learn all the time. You have learnt to do some or all of these things:

■ how to do things round the house, like changing a plug or switching off the water

■ how to look after children

■ how to do your job

■ how to drive

■ how to manage your household expenses

■ how to carry out a particular hobby or interest.

In any of these examples you will have used special skills. In driving or housework these may be practical – using the steering wheel or working the vacuum cleaner. In managing your expenses they will be mental – for example, doing arithmetic. Often, as with looking after children, you use both practical and mental skills, and your emotions as well. You have probably learnt all these skills on your own, or with the help of someone who is not a school or college teacher.

Formal learning, or study, is just another kind of learning. It has its own particular skills, such as reading or writing, which we will look at in detail in this course. But it is still only learning. And one thing is sure: you will have learning strengths that you can build on.

Activity

Think of some things you have learned. You could include examples both of:

■ formal learning – things you learnt at school or college

■ informal learning – things you learnt at home or work.

Select three things that you have enjoyed learning or which you feel have been successful, and three things you have not enjoyed learning or where you have felt unsuccessful.

Fill in the boxes in the table that follows to show why you feel each learning experience was positive or negative. Was it because of:

■ how easy or difficult you found the learning?

■ whether you were interested in what you were learning or not?

■ whether you liked what you were learning?

■ the kind of help you had or did not have?

What you learnt	Why was this?
Enjoyable/successful	
Example 1	
Example 2	
Example 3	
Unenjoyable/unsuccessful	
Example 4	
Example 5	
Example 6	

Comment

Many learners find that the following factors affect how well they learn.

Positive factors	**Negative factors**
You want to learn	Other people tell you to learn
You are interested by the subject	You find the subject boring
You have good support from other people	You have poor support – or none at all
You learn effectively	You learn ineffectively
You have enough time	You are short of time

It makes sense to build on the things you enjoy and do well.

Ways of learning

The last activity asked you to think about ways in which you learn best. This section will take this further. Everyone has their own learning style, and while one style is ideal for one person, another person will learn the same thing in a different way.

For example, you may prefer to:

■ be told what to do, or to decide what to do yourself

■ be left alone to do something, or to work with someone else

■ be very tidy, or quite disorganised.

This activity will help you find out what learning style suits you best.

Activity

Which style suits you best?

1 Look through each of these pairs of statements.

2 For each pair, decide whether Statement A or Statement B is closest to your own feelings. Tick the box nearest that statement.

3 If you really are not sure, tick the middle box.

Statement A				Statement B
I like detailed instructions	❐	❐	❐	I like to try things on my own
I enjoy reading around a subject	❐	❐	❐	I enjoy learning by doing
I prefer my tutor to tell me what to do	❐	❐	❐	I prefer to negotiate what I will do with my tutor
I like to work on my own	❐	❐	❐	I like to work with others
I like to do one thing at a time	❐	❐	❐	I like to have several things on the go at once
I prefer everything to be tidy and organised	❐	❐	❐	I can cope with things being untidy
I need the discipline of a set timetable	❐	❐	❐	I can motivate myself to do things
I think exams reflect my abilities well	❐	❐	❐	I like my progress to be checked as I go along
I need to be prodded into action regularly	❐	❐	❐	I am good at keeping myself motivated
I like to work steadily	❐	❐	❐	I need a challenge
I need a good reason for taking a course	❐	❐	❐	I find out about the course as I go along

Comment

None of these statements is good or bad – they are all strategies for learning that some people use effectively. Some people must keep everything tidy and organised, while others thrive on what looks like chaos. However, you can draw three lessons from what you ticked.

1 In some cases, you will have a tried and tested way of learning that you know works for you – you need to make the most of this.

2 In other cases, you may like to try using a different approach – you may be surprised at how well it suits you.

3 Finally, in some cases you will have to adopt an approach that doesn't suit you – for example you may have to take exams even if you find them stressful. You need to decide what you can do to overcome these problems. This course will help in some cases. And you can always discuss it with your tutor. Or you could talk it over with any friends who are on, or have been on, similar courses to the one you're having problems with.

Research that has been carried out with other learners does suggest that some approaches to learning may be more effective than others.

■ You are more likely to succeed if you take an active approach to learning, question what you do and try to understand it.

■ You are less likely to succeed if you are more passive, do only what other people tell you, and concentrate on remembering things rather than understanding them.

Unit 2, 'Learning effectively', will help you to understand learning better, and to develop strategies that will help you to learn effectively. The section on 'Getting support' at the end of this unit will help you if you feel you need more help from other people.

Here is what some other students on *How to Study Effectively* have said:

> *I need to talk things over with someone or else I just come to a halt. That was the worst problem when I started this course. It's easy to feel isolated. But now I've found a friend who is very good at listening and I meet with her regularly to talk things through.*

> *I always used to work in a muddle, and I honestly felt this suited me best. However, when I tried keeping my desk tidy, I found it actually helped me work more effectively. I wouldn't say I have become fanatical about tidying things up but I make more of an effort now.*

> *As I am self-employed I have got very used to taking my own decisions, and I was nervous that I would always have to do what my tutor told me. In fact, I have been able to discuss and agree my study with her and I find this works very well.*

Reasons for study

There are many different reasons for wanting to study. Some will be your own – to get a better job, to go to university. Others will be other people's reasons – because your manager asks you, for example. It is very important to make the most of your own reasons, as these will keep you motivated for longer.

Your own reasons may be:

■ vocational – related to your work

■ academic – for example, to prepare to study with the Open University

■ personal – for example, to raise your self-esteem or to make better use of your time.

Activity

Think about what you are studying or planning to study. What are your reasons for doing this? Tick any of the reasons below, and add any other factors that may motivate you:

❐ getting a more fulfilling job

❐ getting more pay

❐ getting a chance to move to a better town

❐ feeling more self-confident

❐ playing a greater part in the community

❐ learning something you enjoy

❐ doing something you have always wanted to do

❐ going on to the Open University

❐ impressing your children

❐ other:

❐ other:

❐ other:

❐ other:

Comment

Try to find ways of making these reasons work for you. For example, you could write them down on a poster above the place you study. Tell other people about them, so that they can back you up.

If you found it difficult to list your reasons for studying, what can you do about this? Good motivation is always tied up with interest in the subject. There are many ways of livening up an area of study.

■ Look out for films, and television and radio programmes connected with the subject.

■ Find out how it comes into everyday life.

■ Try reading a book on its history.

■ Try to find out how your subject relates to other subjects.

All these approaches can stimulate your interest and increase your motivation.

If you still find it hard to convince yourself that you have good reasons for studying, talk this over with your tutor or with a friend. It may be that now is not the best time for you to study, or that you have chosen the wrong course. It may be better to reconsider what you are doing now rather than later.

Setting goals

Once you are clear about why you are learning you will have a clear motivation for studying. You know that as long as these reasons don't change, your learning will be worth the effort. However, your reasons are likely to be quite distant and long term. It may take you several months or even years to achieve them. And it's easy to get dispirited along the way.

So it makes sense to set shorter-term goals which will help to keep you going on a day-to-day basis. Most courses are divided up into several modules or units, because most students like a regular sense of getting somewhere. So goals you could set yourself might include:

■ completing a short course or one part of a longer course

■ completing a unit or assignment.

Goals like this are like milestones during a long walk – they give you something to aim at soon, and they give you a regular sense of achievement.

Activity

Begin with this course. When, ideally, would you like to complete it? Many learners take between three and six months, though some go more quickly and others like to spread it over a longer period. Note your target date in the box below.

In the light of this, can you set yourself some shorter-term targets? How quickly will you aim to complete each unit? For example, if you want to complete the course in four months, you will need to do about two units a month, or one every fortnight. Again, note these in the box below.

Target date for completing the course:

Target date for completing Unit 2:
Target date for completing Unit 3:
Target date for completing Unit 4:
Target date for completing Unit 5:
Target date for completing Unit 6:

Obtain a calendar, wall chart or a filofax planning sheet and mark your goals on this.

....

Comment

Don't feel that you have to get this exactly right now. You can always revise your goals later.

Check that your goals take account of times you will be unable to study, such as family holidays, weekends away, times when you are likely to be very busy at work and will have to stay late or bring work home, or school holidays if these are a busy time for you.

A typical month on your study calendar might look like this:

M	T	W	T	F	S	S
1	2	3	4	5	Weekend away 6	6
8	Start Unit 2 9	10	Swimming Gala 11	12	Finish Unit 2 13	14
Start Unit 3 15	Birthday 17	18	Write Assignment C 19	10	20	21
Check Assignment C 22	23	24	25	Post Assignment C 26	27	28

If you are taking other courses at the moment, you should set yourself similar goals for them. Note these in the action plan at the end of the unit.

Planning your work in this way has a number of advantages.

- You ensure that you put in work regularly.

- You don't panic because you have left your work until the last minute.

- Once you have completed the work that you planned for a particular number of days, the rest of the days are free from the worry of not getting your work done.

- By allowing a span of days rather than one day to do your work, you can then cope with unforeseen interruptions.

- By splitting any assignment into three parts (writing it, checking it and posting it), you can allow yourself time to think about what you've written before you go on to the next stage. That way you won't rush it to meet a deadline and then wish you'd changed something after you've posted it.

Key skill

Planning your learning is central to the key skill *Improving your own learning and performance*.

Being realistic

Your goals will only help you if they are realistic. In particular, they need to reflect your learning style; if you are someone who needs a deadline to get you going, make sure you have regular deadlines; if you are someone who likes a challenge, make sure your goals will stretch you enough; and if you are someone who likes being prodded, agree your goals with your tutor or a friend.

Good goals are also:

- achievable – you know you will be capable of meeting them

- reasonable – if you set goals that you cannot meet, they will reduce rather than increase your motivation

- flexible – it is always worth building in some contingency time in case something unpredictable happens, like an illness

- sufficient – at the same time, your goals must ensure that you achieve what you want to do.

It is also important to make the most of your study sessions and to choose study times that reflect your learning style; if you work best in the morning, try to plan morning study sessions. Allow enough time to do something useful each time you study and make the most of the times you set aside; if you tire after one hour, is it really worth setting aside two-hour study periods?

When you study, build in variety; if you blend reading, writing, thinking, research and doing, you can concentrate for longer.

Activity

Ask yourself whether each of these questions is true for you.

	Always	Sometimes	Rarely
Do you achieve what you want to achieve in each study session?	❑	❑	❑
Can you cope if unexpected illness or similar contingencies arise?	❑	❑	❑
Are you allowing enough time to do something useful each time you study?	❑	❑	❑
Are you sure you can make the most of the times you set aside?	❑	❑	❑
Are you building in variety?	❑	❑	❑
Do you study at a good time of day?	❑	❑	❑

Comment

Many people motivate themselves to study by deciding on a goal for a particular day (or evening) and promising themselves a reward when they have finished. This really helps you to get started and not to become easily distracted. Most people find it very hard to study, so do not worry if it is difficult for you. The great Italian dramatist, Alfieri, even made his servant tie him to the study table!

Timetables are great aids to efficiency. They enable you to analyse the use you are making of your time. Is it the most effective scheme? Are the hours allocated to study the best ones? A timetable also takes a load off your mind; without a timetable you will have to make a hundred decisions each week as you try to fit everything in. Timetabling the day's or week's routine ensures that you take all the decisions in advance.

One student found it helpful to produce the following weekly study plan.

Tasks – week beginning 7 March	Time and place
Preview Unit 3	On the train Monday
Do Unit 3 activities	7–9 p.m. Tuesday
Background reading	Lunch hour Wednesday
Do assignment C	7–8 a.m. Thursday
Extra times in case of unforseen interruptions:	Thursday evening Lunch hour Friday

Note down your study plan for next week in the space below.

Tasks – week beginning   **Time and place**

Being positive

Many people feel nervous about learning or may be anxious about how well they will be able to learn something new. Often such feelings go back to childhood and schooling when negative criticism or a sense of failure may have left people feeling unsuccessful or inadequate. However, while such feelings can be strong, they are also wrong – everyone can learn effectively.

There are many ways in which you can build confidence in your own learning.

- **Emphasise the positive**: at the start of this unit you listed some enjoyable and successful things you learnt. Extend this list every time you remember something else or succeed in meeting one of your goals. Write down the list and keep it somewhere you can refer to regularly to reinforce your confidence.

- **Positive self-talk**: you can take this a step further by using a technique called 'healthy self-talk'. To do this you tell yourself out loud that you are good at learning, that you know many valuable things and are still learning all the time. You can even do this in front of a mirror.

- **Eat the elephant**: people on time management courses are often asked 'How can you eat an elephant?' The answer is 'one piece at a time'. It's easy to feel daunted by a major course of study but the answer is just the same – break your learning up into really small steps, set yourself frequent, achievable goals and reward yourself when you achieve them.

- **Experiment**: try out new approaches like the ones we describe in this book. They may not all suit you – but build on the ones that do and put them into regular practice.

It also helps if you can get some positive support from other people, and the last part of this unit looks at how you can do this.

Getting support

Gaining the support of other people, and making the most of them, may be key to your success as a learner. What kinds of support you want from other people – and how much – will depend on your style of learning. For example, some people are very good at sticking to their plans and timetables, while others need regular support if they are to keep going.

Activity

Look through the list of types of support you might need below. For each one, decide whether you think you will need this kind of help, and if so write an example in the space provided. Then think of someone who you might be able to ask to give you this support.

Type of support	Examples	Your example	Person/people to ask
Help with daily tasks	*Looking after children*		
Finding a place to study	*Space at home/work*		
Keeping your morale up	*Someone who can cheer you up*		
Help with planning	*Discussing timetables*		
Testing out ideas	*Brainstorming*		
Explaining things to you	*Showing how something works*		
Talking things through	*Planning a piece of work*		
Reading what you write	*Comments on style, spelling*		
Giving feedback	*Comments on clarity*		
Obtaining information	*Suggesting books to read*		
Other:			
Other:			

Comment

Different people may be able to help you:

- your tutor, teacher, lecturer or trainer
- other people like librarians, technicians
- other learners
- friends, family and colleagues.

And they may be able to help in different ways.

- Your tutor may well be the ideal person to read what you do, give you comments or explain difficult points to you.
- A librarian may be able to help you find information.
- Another learner may be helpful for generating ideas or talking things through.
- A friend might be good at keeping your morale up, while your family might be able to give you practical or emotional support.

You should talk to the people you have identified and discuss how they may be able to help. You will need to:

- arrange a time and place to discuss it with them
- prepare what you will say
- agree how you will work together
- monitor how it is going.

Activity

It is particularly important to prepare what you will say. Note down the names of the people you have identified and beside each name write down any points you would want to cover when you talk to them.

Person	Points to cover
1	
2	
3	

Comment

Points you may want to cover could include:

- describing briefly what you are learning

- explaining your reasons for learning

- checking in principle if they would be prepared to help

- explaining what kind of support you want from them

- discussing practical issues such as how much time might be involved, whether you would need to meet up and how often.

Summary

- You are learning all the time.

- You should build on the things you enjoy and do well.

- Different people can use different learning styles successfully.

- You are more likely to succeed if you take an active approach to learning, question what you do and try to understand it.

- Make sure you have your own reasons for studying, as these will keep you motivated.

- Get a clear overview of your course and set yourself goals and targets.

- Make the most of your study sessions by studying at a good time of day, for the right amount of time.

ACTION PLAN

You may like to note down the main points you have found out here.

I learn best by:

I find the following things difficult:

I will try out the following approaches to see if they suit me better:

I will review my learning style by the following date:

Summarise your main goals for the next six months here.

Date	Course	Target

UNIT TWO

Learning effectively

Introduction

Although much research has been done into learning, we still know surprisingly little about what it involves. And as we said in Unit 1, you are the person who knows most about how you learn. However, experts on learning have highlighted a number of skills and strategies that help us to learn effectively. This unit explores each of these skills in turn and suggests strategies for developing and using them.

Objectives

This unit will help you to:

- concentrate on what you are learning

- use your existing knowledge and experience

- ask questions to help you understand

- be creative and come up with your own ideas

- tackle your study problems

- reflect on what you learn

- identify opportunities to use and develop these skills

- use your memory.

The main skills and strategies that we focus on in this unit are:

- being able to **concentrate** on what you are learning; you will encounter a range of ideas and facts and you need to be able to focus your attention on these fully, and select what is most useful

- linking new ideas and facts to your **existing knowledge and experience** will help you to learn them; you are more likely to be able to remember or apply something if you learn it in context than if you learn it in isolation

- you must work actively on what you are learning; it's important to **ask questions** and seek your own understanding if you are to remember

- you also need to allow time to **be creative**, and to come up with your own ideas; it may well be that some important learning takes place as a result of insights

- adopting a **problem-solving** approach where possible can increase your ability to learn

- **reflecting** on your learning can help you to make the most of it.

This diagram shows how these skills and strategies can work together to help you learn effectively.

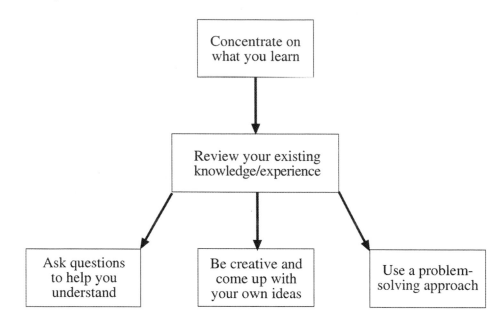

Concentrating

Being able to concentrate is a vital first step in learning. If you are constantly distracted, or if your attention wavers, you will find it hard to get going.

Concentration involves a number of things:

- reducing **interruptions** to a minimum; interruptions come from other people; they could include the television being on in the same room, the children asking questions or the telephone ringing; few people can concentrate effectively under pressures like these!

- clearing your own mind of **distractions;** distractions come from yourself; they could include other things you have to do, or other activities that you would enjoy doing; you may be tempted to do these rather than to study

- being able to **focus your attention** clearly on what you are learning; knowing why you are learning something, and what you want to get out of it.

Activity

What may be stopping you concentrating effectively on your learning? Note down in the space below:

- any regular interruptions to your studying

- distractions that make it hard for you to keep going

- anything else that stops you focusing fully on your learning.

Then think about each item and try to suggest a solution. For example, could you:

- find somewhere else to study?

- make a list of tasks to do each day?

What stops you concentrating   **What you might be able to do**

Interruptions – from others:

Distractions – from yourself:

Anything else:

Comment

Here are some ways of tackling interruptions and distractions.

- Can you negotiate study times with other members of the family?

- Can you identify a better part of the house for studying?

- Could you study elsewhere – in a library, or on the train to work?

- Can you timetable the tasks that get in your way, so that you know you will do them?

- Can you promise yourself time off to do the things you really enjoy?

- Can you use a desk or table where you can leave your books undisturbed, so that it's easy to get started again?

The key to focusing your attention is to make sure you are interested in what you are learning. Your reasons for study and your targets (see Unit 1, 'How do you learn?') should help you to do this. So will the other ideas in this unit.

Using existing knowledge and experience

It's unlikely that much of what you learn will be completely new to you. If you study a subject like History or Economics you can draw on your general knowledge; if you are learning a practical skill you will be influenced by other similar things you can do; and even if you are tackling an abstract topic in Maths, you are likely to use operations you have already learnt.

Research suggests that this is a very good way to learn. For example, one research project found that people learnt about Buddhist ideas much more easily if they linked them to what they already knew about Christianity. It seems that you can understand and remember new facts and ideas far better if you 'attach' them like this to other things you know about and understand already.

However, it's not always obvious how to make the links with what you know or have done already. So how can you do this?

Activity

Imagine that you have to start learning a new topic now – perhaps 'inflation' on an Economics course. Can you suggest at least three ways in which you could link this new topic to what you already know? Write them in the box below.

Comment

Here are some possible ideas.

■ When you start a new topic, write down everything you already know about it. Just reviewing your existing knowledge will help make your mind more receptive to the new material you will meet. For example, if you were learning about inflation as part of an Economics course, you might be surprised at how much you know about the subject already – things like price rises, wage increases and monetarist politicians.

■ Early on in a topic, aim to get an overview of what it is about. You can fit the details into this later. You could try drawing a map of the topic with a key idea in the middle and all the other ideas round the outside. Unit 4, 'Keeping notes', may be helpful here.

- Try to think of examples of what you are learning. For inflation, you could try to find relevant articles in your newspaper or in television news reports; and what about the effect it has on your own spending power or that of the organisation you work for?

- Discuss a topic with other learners and share existing ideas and facts. Try to identify examples together.

- Ask your tutor which of the topics you have already studied relate to the next topic, and review your notes on these first.

- Try to choose textbooks that give good introductions, summaries and regular headings. (See Unit 3, 'Reading'.) You may well find it helps to look at these parts first, to help you gain an overview of the topic.

In fact, this activity was itself an example; just thinking about the question before reading my comment will have helped your mind take in some of the ideas.

Asking questions

All effective learning is active learning. Even if you're reading a book, listening to a talk or looking up an Internet site you need to be active to make the most of it. The key to active learning is asking questions. And you can learn more actively by becoming better at asking questions. Some of the most useful question words are *what*, *why*, *how*, *who*, *where* and *when*.

You can use questions in all kinds of circumstances. For example:

- to focus your approach to a topic

- to help you plan a piece of work

- as headings for notes

- as the basis for an interview with another person such as your tutor

- as the structure of a report or essay plan.

Listed below are the questions one History student wrote as she prepared to study Chamberlain's policy of appeasement.

> *What was appeasement?*
> *What was the background to appeasement?*
> *What other points of view were there at the time?*
> *Why did Chamberlain adopt this policy?*
> *How did he carry out the policy?*
> *How did the policy change?*
> *Who supported Chamberlain's policy? Who opposed him?*
> *When did appeasement start?*
> *When did it become clear that it was not working?*

Activity

Choose a topic that you are studying or planning to study. Aim to write down at least two questions beginning with each of the following words below.

What …

What …

Why …

Why …

How …

How …

Who…

Who …

Where …

Where …

When …

When …

Comment

How easy it was to find questions may depend on the topic. In the History example we looked at it was harder to find 'where' questions than 'what' questions. So don't worry if you found it easier to think of some questions than others.

Once you have thought of the questions, the next stage is of course to answer them. Some you will already know the answer to, or have some ideas about. In other cases you will need to do more research, perhaps by asking someone else or by reading about it.

You may like to go back to the questions you wrote down and tick the ones you can answer now. Beside the others, write in the name of someone you could ask, a place to visit or a book to consult.

Being creative

Learning, like most things, usually involves 10 per cent inspiration and 90 per cent perspiration. However, that 10 per cent of the time when you need to be inspired and creative will be critical to your success the other 90 per cent of the time. You may need to be creative when:

■ you begin to plan a project

■ you are starting a piece of writing

■ you feel dissatisfied with what you are doing

■ you get stuck.

It's easy to think that you are not a creative person, but in practice everyone can be creative. Being creative isn't simply about writing plays or music; it's also about enriching the quality of your learning and experiences by being able to:

■ stand back from your day-to-day tasks and routines

■ put your preconceptions out of your mind

■ examine things from different perspectives

■ welcome strange ideas

■ cope with being uncertain for a time.

One of the best ways of being creative is brainstorming. To brainstorm, you write down a word or phrase (it could be an assessment question) on a piece of blank paper, and spend a few minutes writing down all the ideas that come into your mind about this word or phrase.

Brainstorming is often used by groups of people, and if you can do it with someone else, great. But you can also do it on your own. This activity will show you how to do it. You'll be amazed at how many ideas you can come up with.

You can brainstorm about absolutely anything. Common examples used in management training include uses of a brick or a paperclip. I suggest you brainstorm all the things that will help you study effectively – though you could choose something else that is more important to you now.

Activity

Here are the four rules.

1   Make sure you won't be interrupted.

2   Spend 10–15 minutes thinking of absolutely anything that could help you study effectively.

3   Write down all your ideas in the space below, even if they seem ridiculous – they may spark off other, useful ideas.

4   If you run out of ideas, try something different – like changing your position in the room or imagining you are someone else.

to study effectively

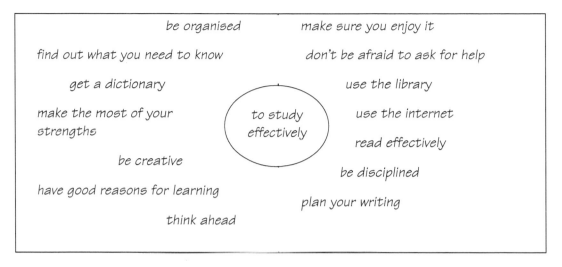

Comment

Here is the result of my own brainstorm about this topic.

> be organised   make sure you enjoy it
>
> find out what you need to know   don't be afraid to ask for help
>
> get a dictionary   use the library
>
> make the most of your   (to study   use the internet
> strengths   effectively)
>   read effectively
>
> be creative
>   be disciplined
>
> have good reasons for learning
>   plan your writing
>
> think ahead

When you have finished your brainstorm, leave it for a while. Then come back and highlight or underline all the ideas that seem useful.

Solving problems

It's normal to run into problems from time to time during your study. The vital thing is to have a good problem-solving procedure so that you can clear them up quickly and make sure they do not become worse.

There are four key stages to problem solving.

1   **Analyse the problem**. The first stage is to spend time thinking the problem through.

    Ask yourself:

    ■   What exactly is it that you have to solve?

    ■   Is it your problem?

    ■   What do you want to achieve?

2   **Obtain information** you need in order to solve it. The next stage is to make sure that you have the relevant details. Just obtaining information can sometimes solve the problem.

    Ask yourself:

    ■   Which books might help?

    ■   Which other resources, such as the library or the Internet, might you try?

    ■   Who can you ask for advice?

3   **Consider alternative solutions** and evaluate each one. When you're faced with a problem, the choices often seem stark. But there may be other possible ways of looking at it, and one way is likely to be more appropriate than the others.

Ask yourself:

- What will be the advantages of each?

- What would be the drawbacks?

- Which will be most appropriate?

4 **Implement the best solution**. Once you have decided, act on it at once, before the problem gets worse.

Activity

Think of any problem you have at the moment, in your study, your work or elsewhere in your life, and practise solving it now.

In the space on the next page:

- describe the problem

- note down what information would help you to solve it

- list some possible solutions

- decide which you feel is the best solution.

Statement of problem:		
Information required: Resources: People:		
Alternative solutions	Advantages	Drawbacks
1		
2		
3		
Chosen solution: Action:		

Comment

The response from one student is shown below.

Statement of problem:		
I am concerned that I will not complete all the course in time and will therefore perform poorly in the exam.		

Information required:

Resources: *obtain copies of syllabus and past exam papers*

People: *talk with tutor*

Alternative solutions	Advantages	Drawbacks
1 Defer exam to next year	Time to prepare Reduced stress	Time lost Extra cost
2 Concentrate on key topics	Stay on schedule Meet other commitments	Fewer questions to choose from Likely lower grade
3 Increase time devoted to study	Full range of questions to answer Stay on schedule	Increased stress Less time for family
Chosen solution:	Concentrate on key topics	
Action:	Discuss further with tutor	

Reflecting on what you learn

Taking a little time to reflect on what you learn is one of the most important ways of benefiting from learning. It can help you in several ways.

■ It gives you a chance to think about *how* you learnt – this means you can weigh up what worked well, and use this in the future.

■ It helps you to remember *what* you learnt.

■ It gives you *time* to plan your next steps.

The research suggests that people develop reflection skills over time. In the early stages, most people need to make time when they consciously reflect on what they have just achieved – this is called 'reflection on action'. As they become more experienced at it, they are able to reflect on things while they are happening – this is called 'reflection in action'.

A good way to develop your reflective skills is to use a diary or learning log. This involves recording what you learn in terms of:

- the experience – a brief summary of what you did.

- your reflection – what you feel you have learnt from this.

- actions – what you might do as a result.

Activity

Use the box below to reflect on a recent experience that you feel you may have learnt from. It could be something to do with this course, or something else in your work or home life.

Begin by writing a short description of the experience. Then reflect on the experience and write down why you felt it was significant. Explain what you learned and how you felt about it. If appropriate, note down any actions you intend to take as a result.

Experience:

What I learnt:

Actions I could take:

Comment

You can use this approach to record and reflect on what you learn:

- in your study

- at work

- in your home and family life.

You may prefer to write your entries in a diary – or just to note down your reflections on sheets of paper as a 'learning log'.

Using your memory

Our memories are very complex and we have only a limited understanding of how they work. However, we do know some important things about memory.

- The research suggests that 20–40 minutes after starting a study session, you reach a peak when you are able both to recall and understand what you are learning. Before this you are still getting into the swing of learning – after it you tend to remember less.

- Certain events or associations appear to trigger our memories – for example, we may recall more at the start and end of a study period than in the middle. We also may be more likely to remember items which are unique or unusual.

- We also appear initially to store knowledge in a short-term memory before transferring it to a longer-term memory.

You can take advantage of these things to make your memory work better for you.

- Firstly, if you take short breaks in a study period, you are more likely to remember what you learn. You will need to work out how long is the best time for you but it is likely to be between 20 and 40 minutes.

- Secondly, you can also increase what you remember by using review techniques which help you to transfer what you learn into your long-term memory. Aim for several reviews.

- Spend about 10 minutes on a **first review** at the end of a one-hour learning period. Review and revise your notes and reflect on what you have learnt. This will keep your recall level high for about a day.

- Next day, spend 2–4 minutes on a **second review**. Jot down on a piece of paper everything you remember, then check this against your notes and make any corrections or additions.

- After a month, do a quick **final review** to store what you have learnt in your long-term memory. Use the same technique as for the second review.

- Use mnemonics to help you to remember something more easily by using association. Typical mnemonics include rhymes; picturing something in your mind; or using the first letters of words to make another word – like 'every good boy deserves favour' for the violin strings EGBDF.

For more on memory see the NEC publication (Leach, *How to improve your memory*). See the *Further reading* section at the end of this book for more details.

Summary

- To learn effectively you must concentrate on what you are learning.

- Aim to link new ideas to existing knowledge.

- Ask questions to help you understand.

- Everyone can be creative.

- A problem-solving approach can increase your ability to learn.

- It is important to reflect on what you learn.

- It is possible to improve your memory.

In this unit you have thought about and practised a number of key learning skills. Using these regularly will greatly increase your success as a learner. However they are all skills that you can develop and improve. The following action plan asks you to identify opportunities to practise and develop them in your study.

ACTION PLAN

Beside each of the skills listed below, think of at least one occasion when you will need to use it. For example:

- you may wish to organise your resources for a forthcoming project

- you could draw up a list of questions for your tutor

- you may need to be creative when you write an essay, assignment or report

- you may need to practise problem solving if you find you are short of time to study.

Note your example in the box below. Then review this over the coming days or weeks and tick each skill as you practise it.

Skill	Occasion	Tick
Concentrating		❑
Using existing knowledge and experience		❑
Asking questions		❑
Being creative		❑
Solving problems		❑

UNIT THREE

Reading

Introduction

Reading is a central task for many learners. The key to successful reading is to decide what to read, to know why you are reading it, and then to select an appropriate strategy for reading it.

This unit will help you to practise a number of strategies so that you learn to read more efficiently.

Objectives

This unit will help you to:

■ list the kinds of reading you will do

■ identify the purpose of your reading

■ identify different reading strategies

■ select appropriate strategies

■ apply appropriate strategies.

Key skill

Reading is one of the main elements of the key skill *Communication.*

Reasons for reading

During your study you may draw on various publications, including:

■ textbooks

■ reference books such as directories, dictionaries and manuals

■ newspapers, magazines and journals

■ literature, including novels, plays and poems

■ material from the Internet

■ other sources such as maps or historical information.

You are likely to consult different publications for different reasons. You might wish to look up a piece of information in a reference book, or you might use a textbook to find the answer to a question that is raised during your course. Your reasons for reading will have a major impact on how you read.

Activity

Note down below six things you read recently. If possible, include some items connected with your study. Beside each item, note down why you were reading it.

Item of reading	Your reason for reading it
1	
2	
3	
4	
5	
6	

Comment

It's likely that you had a variety of reasons, which could have included:

■ obtaining a particular piece of information – for example, the price of an item in a catalogue, a list of bed and breakfasts from the Internet, the meaning of a word in a dictionary, or the date of a historical event

■ finding the answer to a question – for example, how to highlight a word in your wordprocessing program, or which character gave a particular speech in a play you are studying

■ gaining more detailed information – for example, the day's news in the paper, or a list of factors affecting bacterial growth

■ trying to understand something – for example, a scientific theory or the reasons why the world went to war in 1914

■ pleasure – for example, a novel, poem or autobiography.

Your purpose will affect the way you read. You might read a novel from cover to cover, you might look for particular articles in a newspaper, and you might just look for one word in a dictionary.

Choosing what you will read

There are numerous ways to find out what to read, including following your tutor's recommendations, a course booklist, other learners' recommendations, bibliographies in other books, library catalogues and the advice of librarians.

If you are following a set course of study, there will almost certainly be some books which are compulsory reading. In addition to these, there will probably be a list of recommended books. It is very unlikely that you will have time to study more than a small section from the list, so you must choose the books with care.

Buy or borrow?

You will also need to decide whether to buy or borrow publications. It is probably worth buying publications that you will need to refer to often during the course of your learning. These might include compulsory texts, reference books, a dictionary, thesaurus and important magazines.

You may prefer to use the library to borrow books you will only need for short periods, for example for a particular assignment. Whether you buy or borrow you will need to plan well ahead. Bookshops often do not stock the books you need and will have to order them for you. Similarly, library books you want to borrow will often be on loan and to avoid this you will have to book them well in advance. You may sometimes have to try two or three libraries for particular texts.

Evaluating a book

Here is a checklist for finding out quickly whether or not a publication is relevant and likely to be useful.

- Do the title, introduction and contents page relate to the topic you are studying?

- Is the author a recognised authority on the subject, or is there a section in the book which tells you the author's credentials?

- When was it published? Is it sufficiently up-to-date?

- Where was it published? Is it relevant to your own country?

- Has your tutor mentioned the publication favourably?

- Is the bibliography comprehensive and up-to-date?

Your own library

Ideally, you should aim to build up a small collection of books in your subject. This can be a very expensive process, so be on the look-out for book sales, second hand bookshops and ex-students wishing to sell their books. Although books are expensive, bear in mind that your collection will save you many trips to libraries and your books will be available whenever you need to refer to them.

How will you read?

Skilled readers vary their reading speed and method to suit both the material they are reading and their purpose in reading it. You 'read' a telephone directory rather differently from a novel. In your learning, you should seek to use a similarly varied approach to reading. Here are some of the main techniques you can use:

- **Skimming:** this involves looking quickly through the book and reading only things like contents, headings, introductions and conclusions. It is a quick and efficient way of familiarising yourself with a publication. It is useful if you wish to check whether a book is relevant or for finding particular information or ideas quickly.

- **Scanning:** this is a very rapid search for some important point. It may be a page number, a title or a key word. The essential thing is that you deliberately ignore everything except the one item for which you are scanning. You use scanning when you look up a number in the telephone directory.

- **Reading to understand:** this involves detailed study of a chapter, passage or article in order to absorb all the major facts and ideas. You may read it more than once and take notes to summarise what you have read.

- **Word by word reading:** very occasionally, you actually need to read every word extremely carefully; for example, when reading an exam question or following a set of instructions.

- **Reading for pleasure:** this is the reading you do to relax and enjoy, as with a novel.

Activity

Look back to the items you mentioned in the first activity in this unit, and your purpose for reading them. Which of the techniques we have just mentioned would be most suited to each one?

Item   **Technique to use**

Comment

Skimming is particularly useful for finding your way round a publication. You may skim the newspaper to find the articles you want to read, or a text book to identify a relevant chapter.

Scanning is useful when you want to identify a particular piece of information – for example, in finding a telephone number or a football result.

Reading to understand is useful when you want to study something thoroughly.

You will probably rarely need word-by-word reading, unless you frequently refer to technical manuals or scientific formulas.

Reading for pleasure could cover any reading – books, newspapers, magazines – which you do for relaxation.

To study efficiently you must learn to vary your reading style to suit both the material in front of you and your reason for reading that material. You must first aim at mastering each type of reading in your studies and, if speed is important to you, in your leisure reading.

By developing the ability to switch from one method of reading to another, you will vastly increase your efficiency. You will be able to search for specific items by scanning, to assess a passage quickly by skimming, and then to read it closely to understand it.

The next three sections look in more detail at skimming, scanning and reading to understand.

Skimming

As we have seen, skimming involves looking quickly through a publication to familiarise yourself with its contents. This activity will help you to practise skimming.

Activity

Practise skimming on this course book. Spend up to ten minutes skimming the remaining units, and aim to find out as much about them as you can. You can check:

■ the contents

■ the introductions and summaries

■ headings and sub-headings in the text

■ first and last paragraphs (or sections) of units; first and last sentences of paragraphs

■ figures and diagrams.

Note what you have found out about the book.

Comment

Your skim should have given you a good idea of what each unit was about – the contents, introductions and objectives will have highlighted what you will get out of each unit, and the headings will have described the ground that each unit covers.

After skimming material in this way you have three choices:

■ decide the publication is not suitable.

■ decide that certain sections are appropriate to your needs.

■ decide that you need to read all of it – even in this case your skimming has still been useful as it has given you an overall view of the material.

Scanning

Scanning involves looking through a publication for a particular piece of information. You may have to scan books or notes for a point to include in your writing, or you may have to scan periodicals and indexes for subjects which are important to your studies.

Activity

Give yourself three minutes to find out the following information about this book.

■ Where is the *Further reading* section?

■ On what page does the heading *Reasons for study* appear?

■ How many times was the word 'skim' used in the last section?

■ Is there a book on memory techniques in *Further reading*?

Comment

Effective scanning involves:

■ using references – the contents page, and the index, if the book has one, will help you find something quickly – you probably used the contents to check where *Reasons for study* appeared

■ moving round the book quickly – just flicking through the book, looking at headings and sub-headings, may help you locate the information you need – this may well be the technique you use to find the weather page in the newspaper

■ using your experience – you may well have expected that the *Further reading* section was at the back, and you were probably able to find the section on *Skimming* without checking the contents page.

Reading to understand

When you need to study something in depth, try using a technique called SQ3R. Don't be put off by the title – it is simply short for:

■ Survey

■ Question

■ Read

■ Recall

■ Review.

This is a simple and useful method of approaching a passage, such as a chapter of a book, which you want to study and master. The idea is that your reading of the passage is broken down into five stages. The details of each stage are given below.

Survey

This is rather like the skimming process. You look at:

■ the title, author, date of first publication and date of this edition, to check that it is relevant to you and up-to-date

■ the contents and chapter headings to identify which parts to concentrate on

■ the introduction, to understand the author's intention in writing the publication

■ the index and bibliography.

Question

Before embarking on detailed reading of all or part of the publication, ask yourself what you expect to gain from it. Why are you reading it? What points are you particularly interested in? These sorts of question ensure that you read with a purpose.

You might even ask, 'Is it worth reading?' To answer this, read its first and last paragraphs, then its first and last sections or chapters. This should help you decide whether it is worth studying.

Read

Begin by getting a clear picture of what the passage is about. You may wish to read a chapter at least twice at a fair speed. Ask yourself the following questions.

■ What is the author's general stance for this passage?

■ What is the basic idea in each paragraph?

■ Do you understand everything the author is saying?

Then look at the detail.

- Which parts are factual? Are all the facts you need provided?

- Which parts give the author's ideas? What evidence does the author produce to back up his or her ideas?

- Look at the examples, diagrams and illustrations. Why did the author choose these examples? What points do they illustrate? Can you think of any contrary examples?

Then form an overall judgement on the passage.

- Is the passage convincing?

- Are there alternative theories which would do just as well in the circumstances?

- What consequences flow from the author's theory? What consequences flow from your alternative theories?

You will notice that at the beginning of the read stage, you are simply trying to grasp what the author says, to understand his or her arguments. Only when you completely follow the author's case do you turn to criticising it. If you criticise too soon, you may not take in everything the author has to say.

Recall

This stage may follow the read stage for the whole passage or, if the passage is rather lengthy or complex, it may follow the read stage for sections of the passage.

The recall stage involves trying to recall all the main ideas in the section you've just read. You may like to write them down in note form (see Unit 4, *Keeping notes*).

Review

The review is the checking stage which follows recall. Look back over the passage and check that your recall was correct. Make a special note of any important points which you failed to recall, or which you wrongly recalled.

Activity

Try practising the SQ3R technique on a passage you are studying. It could be a chapter from a book or an article from a journal or magazine. Or you can use the newspaper article on the next page. Apply the following SQ3R technique to the passage.

1 Survey the passage.

2 Question. Write down the questions you hope to be able to answer by reading the chapter.

3 Read.

4 Recall. Jot down the answers to your questions.

5 Review what you have jotted down by referring back to your questions.

Sample article for reading practice

Half of us could be short-sighted soon – and it may be an evolutionary consequence of modern lifestyles. **Roger Dobson** looks at a worrying development.

Myopia is now one of the world's biggest epidemics. Tens of millions of people suffer from short sight and it has been predicted that half the world's population will soon be myopic.

In Britain, one in three people is short-sighted, and in parts of the Far East more than 90 per cent of university graduates are sufferers. In Singapore, the problem is so acute that the air force has had problems in recruiting flyers, because of a lack of graduates who can meet the necessary vision requirements.

'The increase has been dramatic in some areas, to a point where the vast majority of the population is now short-sighted,' says Dr Flitcroft, an ophthalmologist who has carried out research into the focusing mechanism of the eye.

'Eighty five per cent of school-children in Taiwan are short-sighted. In Singapore, they had to alter the regulations covering short sight in the air force because by the time they graduated and completed five years of training, recruits were short-sighted. In the US, the latest study shows that it is heading towards 45 per cent. That compares to about 20 per cent in the earlier part of the century, and studies of families have also shown that the younger siblings tend to have more myopia. In parts of the Far East where eye tests are compulsory at 18, it's been found that the prevalence of myopia is increasing in less than a generation.

No one really knows why this increase is occurring, although there are various theories. The dominant view is that the modern lifestyle, with its demands for close work, is to blame. The latest suggestion is that exposure to nightlights in infancy may be responsible for physical changes in the eye. Another theory is that myopia is an evolutionary inevitability, and that the eye is adapting to changing circumstances.

In the past, man's dominant need was for good distance vision, but with eight or more hours a day now spent in close work, the eye is giving priority to near sight.

Short sight occurs when the curvature of the cornea is too steep or the eyeball is too long. As a result, light rays come to a focus in front of the retina rather than on it, as it would with perfect vision. The myopic sees near objects clearly, but distant images are blurred.

It was once thought that short sight was solely an inherited problem. Genetic factors do play a role, but the trigger for most myopia is now considered to be an environmental one. That would explain why the rates of myopia in Britain soar from 2 per cent in five-year-olds to up to 40 per cent in adults.

The finger of suspicion points at close work, in particular reading, and the increased use of PCs and computer games. The move towards sedentary pursuits means that children are spending less time playing sports and games, which require distant vision, and this compounds the problem.

A study of Eskimos found that the number of people with myopia increased from 2 per cent in one generation to 45 per cent in the next generation. There had been no changes in diet or lifestyle, but the researchers concluded that their deteriorating eyesight was due to a shift in educational practices. The oral tradition of Eskimo schooling had been replaced by formal, written education, with several hours a day of reading and writing.

Another survey, of Orthodox Jews, found that men had much higher rates of myopia than women. This was blamed on the fact that the men spent several hours a day, from an early age, reading religious texts (and the women didn't).

It is now thought that there may be some kind of trigger mechanism that makes the eye grow longer in response to the demand of close work, and it doesn't take long for harmful effects to occur. A British study revealed that workers who spent eight hours a day looking at samples through microscopes became myopic after just two years.

'The researchers measured the eye lengths of these adults when they started the job, and went back a few years later and a third of them had become myopic; their eyes had ended up too long. Within two years, the eyes had started to change,' said Dr Ian Flitcroft.

'There is no doubt that near work is much the most intuitively plausible explanation,'confirms Dr Richard Wormald, an ophthalmic epidem-iologist and consultant surgeon at Moorfields Eye Hospital. 'Human beings are extraordinarily adaptive to their environment, and if you spend most of your time focusing on near objects the eye will adapt. The amount of time children spend studying has increased compared with even a few years ago.'

Much of the research has concentrated on the Far East, because of the high rates of myopia in urban populations compared with rural areas. 'What is different and quite remarkable about the Far East is the amount of school work done by children, six hours at school and another six hours' homework. Teenage homework diaries there are quite outrageous,' says Dr Ian Flitcroft. 'The highest incidence of myopia ever recorded was in Singapore, where 98 per cent of medical graduates were found to be myopic. We know that only about 2 per cent of children are myopic at the age of five, so that is a huge increase.

The latest theory, from the Philadelphia Children's Hospital, is that nightlights can damage your eyes. Children who have nightlights during their first two years were up to five times more likely to be myopic. Researchers are not certain why, and the results may have been confounded by other factors. Parents who give their children nightlights, for example, may be more likely to encourage them to read and study, too. Fearful children who need nightlights may also be more imaginative and more likely to be avid readers.

Myopia is currently alleviated with contact lenses, glasses or corrective surgery, and each option has its drawbacks. Any surgery has associated risks, and there are no guarantees that the eye will not deteriorate again later.

Contact lenses are not suitable for small children, and may leave the eye vulnerable to infections if they are not correctly handled. Glasses will not cure deficiencies and may even worsen the existing complaint. It has been suggested that using spectacles as a visual aid thwarts the eye's own corrective processes.

Studies have shown that if an animal with normal eyesight is given glasses, its eyes will adjust so that when the glasses are removed the animal has become myopic.

However, new research being carried out in America may offer a preventive solution and help to reverse the current trend. Researchers have recruited 469 children aged from six to 11, half of whom will wear special bifocal glasses for the next three years. It is hoped that these will prevent their eyes from changing shape. If successful, it could fundamentally change the way we use glasses. Instead of being a visual aid, they could offer a cure for myopia.

Source: Roger Dobson, 'The Thursday Review', *The Independent*, 20 May 1999.

Activity

To help you in your reading, it is useful to know something about how writing is usually structured. In particular, this will help you to find your way around paragraphs quickly and identify which paragraphs are relevant to you.

Paragraphs generally cover one main idea, and you can usually find this idea in what is called a 'topic sentence'. For example, the sentence you have just read is the topic sentence of this paragraph, and the main idea is 'paragraphs generally cover one idea'. All the other sentences are likely to support this main idea, perhaps by giving examples or extending the idea further.

Look back to the section of this course on *Being creative* in Unit 2, *Learning effectively*. There are five paragraphs in the introduction to this section. Can you identify the main idea and the topic sentence in each paragraph?

Paragraph 1:

Paragraph 2:

Paragraph 3:

Paragraph 4:

Paragraph 5:

Comment

The main idea in the first paragraph is that creativity is important in learning. So the topic sentence is the second one which begins 'However, that 10 per cent of the time...'. The rest of the paragraph just gives examples.

The main idea in the second paragraph is that everyone can be creative, so the topic sentence this time is the first one, beginning 'It's easy to think...'.

In the third paragraph the first sentence is again the topic sentence and the main idea is that brainstorming is a good way to be creative.

I think the main idea of the fourth paragraph is that the activity will show you how to do it – in which case the topic sentence is the third one, beginning 'This activity will...'. But you might argue that the fact that brainstorming can be done in groups is the main idea.

Finally, the first sentence of the last paragraph is again probably the topic sentence, and the main idea is that you can brainstorm almost anything.

This activity should have helped you identify the ideas in paragraphs. It has also shown that the topic sentence is often the first one.

Reading quickly

Reading quickly is much less important than reading effectively. Many people who feel they read slowly actually use the wrong reading strategies – they may read right through a book without concentrating on the parts that matter. If you practise skimming, scanning and SQ3R, you will become an efficient reader and you will also start to read more quickly.

However, you may wish to improve your reading speed still further. It can actually be difficult to get a reliable indication of the speed at which you read. If the material is familiar, if the vocabulary is simple, and/or if you are interested, you tend to read faster. And beware of speed-reading teachers who simplify the material in order to produce good results in their students!

If you wish to get a rough indication of your reading speed, try the following activity.

Activity

1   Find a passage of familiar material (the one you used for the previous activity would be suitable).

2   Read from the start at your normal speed (not aloud) for one minute.

3   Count the number of words you have read.

4   Repeat steps 2 and 3 twice, starting at different points.

Comment

If your reading speed is below 200 words per minute you may be able to increase it as follows:

■   Decide on your purpose before you start and concentrate on this.

■   Always skim new material first and scan for key words and ideas.

■   Train your eyes to see more in each eye movement. Instead of moving them along each line of print concentrate on the centre of each line.

■   Do not look back after you have read a difficult sentence. Keep going and see if the meaning becomes clearer. If necessary, go back when you have finished the section.

■   Avoid mouthing the words. The way to overcome this is to read faster than you can speak.

See the Further reading list for further guidance on reading skills.

Using a dictionary

If you don't have a dictionary, or if you feel your current dictionary is not very helpful, you may need to buy a different one. The *Pocket Oxford Dictionary* is one that many students use.

A dictionary entry will look something like the central box below. Your dictionary will contain a key which explains the system of symbols or abbreviations it uses. They may be a little different from those in the example.

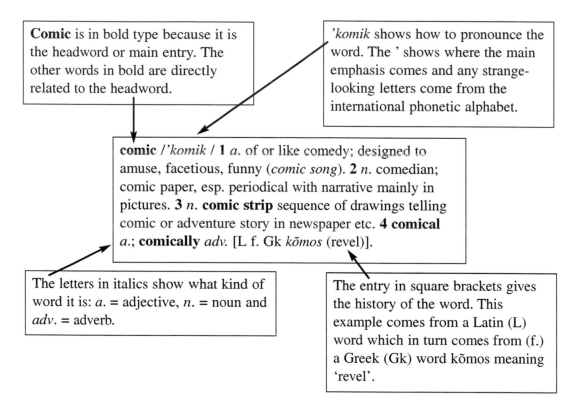

Comic is in bold type because it is the headword or main entry. The other words in bold are directly related to the headword.

'komik shows how to pronounce the word. The ' shows where the main emphasis comes and any strange-looking letters come from the international phonetic alphabet.

comic */'komik / 1 a.* of or like comedy; designed to amuse, facetious, funny (*comic song*). **2** *n.* comedian; comic paper, esp. periodical with narrative mainly in pictures. **3** *n.* **comic strip** sequence of drawings telling comic or adventure story in newspaper etc. **4 comical** *a.*; **comically** *adv.* [L f. Gk *kõmos* (revel)].

The letters in italics show what kind of word it is: *a.* = adjective, *n.* = noun and *adv.* = adverb.

The entry in square brackets gives the history of the word. This example comes from a Latin (L) word which in turn comes from (f.) a Greek (Gk) word kõmos meaning 'revel'.

Many words have more than one meaning, and it is always important to check that you have chosen the right definition. For example, in the following sentences, the word 'easy' has two different meanings. Look up 'easy' in your dictionary and see if you can find the two meanings there.

■ He is an easy person to persuade

■ She has a very easy manner.

Summary

- Reading is a central task to most learners.

- Your purpose for reading should influence how you read.

- You should adopt different reading methods.

- You don't always have to read every word – skimming and scanning are also useful techniques for obtaining information.

- A useful method for reading to understand is SQ3R – survey, question, read, recall and review.

- Reading effectively is more important than reading quickly.

- Dictionaries are an invaluable aid to reading.

ACTION PLAN

Summarise your work on this unit here. Note down:

- what you need to read for your course

- why you need to read it

- how you will read it.

What you need to read	Why you need to read it	How you will read it

UNIT FOUR

Keeping notes

Introduction

Your own notes can be some of the most useful aids to your study. They can help you to understand what you are learning and to remember it later.

In this unit we look at why you might need to make notes, and at how useful your existing note-making is. We then go on to examine different methods of note-making and to consider ways of storing your notes.

Finally, the unit concludes by looking at two important sources of information: the library and the Internet.

Objectives

This unit will help you to:

■ list the kinds of notes and other records you should keep

■ identify the purpose of your notes/records

■ identify different ways of making notes

■ analyse your notes

■ make effective notes

■ obtain information from the library and the Internet.

Why take notes?

You may need to take notes for a number of reasons:

■ to help you **remember** something: you can't hope to retain a whole lecture, book, web site or discussion permanently in your memory, so instead you make notes of the most important items and use the notes for revision and reference

■ to keep a **permanent record** of something: if you attend a lecture or visit somewhere as part of your course, your notes may be your only record of what took place

- to help in your **planning**: notes can be a good way of starting off a project or a piece of writing; you can note down the main things you need to do, the books you will read, and so on

- to **re-order material**: making notes is one of the most useful opportunities for rearranging material in whichever form is most convenient to you

- to help you **understand** what you are learning: writing things down yourself forces you to think them through properly and is one of the best ways of remembering them

- to help you to **concentrate**: if you are listening to someone talking, your mind may easily wander; making notes helps to keep you active and involved

- to provide **evidence**: if you seek a National Vocational Qualification (NVQ) or similar certificate, you may need to provide notes to prove that you have done something

- to **show other people**: you may want other learners to benefit from the notes you have made.

Activity

Look through three examples of notes you have made for your study. Note down here what they were about, and why you made them.

Notes	Why you made them

Comment

Your reasons for taking notes are very important. For example, if other people will read your notes – and especially if they will assess them as evidence – they may need to be more detailed or tidy than if you are the only person who will read them. If they will be your only permanent record, they will need to be self-contained, whereas if they are based on a book you own, you can always cross-refer to particular passages in the book.

Your reasons will also affect the way you make notes. You may well wish to concentrate on written notes; most learners do. Written notes are easy to make, and you can easily access them later. But bear in mind the alternatives.

- If you have a wordprocessor, could you use this? It would have the advantage that you could easily modify notes and rearrange them.

- Could you use a tape recorder in some circumstances? It might be a useful way of recording your first ideas. Bear in mind that if you record what someone else says, it is wise to ask their permission.

Finally, the purpose of your notes may affect the kind of notes you take. We will look at different types of notes later in the unit.

How useful are your notes?

Notes are usually a personal learning aid, so the most important thing about them is that they suit your learning style and your reasons for taking them.

Above all, notes should be:

- brief and clear: if they are too long, you will find it tedious to wade through them, either to look for a specific point, or to refresh your memory

- easy to read and understand: if you cannot quickly read through them to refresh your memory, they will fail in their purpose

- organised to suit the way you learn and your reasons for learning: if they are not relevant to you, you will never look at them again.

....

Activity

Look at each of the sets of notes you used in the previous activity, and tick whether they are:

Easy to read	❏	❏	Difficult to read
Brief	❏	❏	Long
Clear	❏	❏	Unclear
Easily understood	❏	❏	Difficult to understand
Organised the way you learn	❏	❏	Organised in some other way
Relevant to your needs	❏	❏	Not relevant to your needs

....

Comment

Have you given yourself lots of ticks in the left-hand column? If you have, then your note-taking system is already excellent. But if you have lots of ticks in the right-hand column, then you need a new approach to note-taking.

The next two sections look at some of the specific points to bear in mind when taking notes from books, articles and speech – talks, lectures, television programmes, interviews, visits, and so forth.

Taking notes from written sources

When taking notes from books and other written sources remember the following points.

Checklist

1   Prepare note-taking by asking yourself what you want to get out of the book, and checking that the book will help you answer these questions.

2   Label your notes clearly. Write down the source. For a book record the:

   ■ title

   ■ author

   ■ publisher and place of publication

   ■ ISBN number and date.

   If it is from a library, also write down the classification number (printed at the base of the spine) for future reference.

3   Get an overall sense of what the book is about, and by skimming see which parts of the book are most relevant. Use the SQ3R technique (see Unit 3, *Reading*) to find out the main points in the chapters.

4   Make notes in your own words. The process of converting the ideas into your own language also ensures that you understand the material. In making permanent notes you will want to do your own rearranging of the material, and possibly you will want to add your own comments and cross-references to other notes.

5   Record the main topics and then note the important points under each topic. These will tend to be headings or brief statements. Where an argument, proof or sequence of reasoning is presented, try to note down the main steps but don't leave out so much that you can't restate the missing processes.

   You should also record the major conclusions or results of each chapter. Thus your framework might be something like this:

   ■ chapter heading

   ■ important points

   ■ illustrations and arguments to support points

   ■ result/conclusions.

   Of course, you shouldn't regard this as a skeleton outline for all note-taking, but it does illustrate the *type* of organisation you should be aiming at when making notes.

6   Record the page numbers of the sections you are noting. For instance 'Brown – p27' means that the notes came from page 27 of Brown's book. In this way you can double-check a point subsequently if you need to. Always remember to put quotation marks around material which you copy exactly from a book – if you have a wordprocessor, you could use it to record quotations. You can then use your quotation (with an appropriate acknowledgement) in your writing without having to return to the original page to check details. This can save you a lot of time.

Note that in some modern examinations – called 'open book exams' – you are allowed to take books into the exam room with you. This can have important implications for how you make notes. For example, you might like to use a blank page in the book to note where key passages or sections of the book are to be found.

Taking notes from speech

Another common occasion for taking notes is to record what someone else has said, perhaps in a talk, lecture or television programme, or during a visit or interview. These notes will be different from those you take from print because you are likely to have just one opportunity to make them, whereas you can read a book at your own pace. So you may have to make hasty notes that you revise afterwards – unless you can tape-record what is said (and you will need the speaker's permission to do this).

Checklist

1   Prepare yourself beforehand by finding out about the topic. This will make it easier to understand and help you to recognise the main points. Note down questions that you want answers to. Make sure you can see and hear the speaker(s) easily.

2   Label your notes clearly. Write down:

- the subject

- the speaker's name

- the date.

3   Try to get a good overall picture of what is being said. Concentrate on understanding first – don't let taking notes get in the way of grasping what is being said. If in doubt, concentrate on listening rather than writing.

4   People do not always stick to a logical order when they talk. You may have to keep order in your notes by using headings that you can go back to if need be.

5   Be prepared to ask questions if you do not understand every point, or if you need further information.

6   Go over your notes as soon as possible afterwards, before the detail fades from memory. If your notes are still confused, talk about them to another student. This may help to clarify them.

If you are attending a course of lectures, and you find that two or three of you are confused, go to see the lecturer concerned. You may be embarrassed about doing this but your study is too important to be ignored. Provided you are reasonably courteous, this strategy often results in the lecturer agreeing to put headings on the whiteboard or use transparencies to clarify important points.

Different types of notes

There is more than one way of making notes, and it makes sense to choose a method or methods which you feel at ease with and which suits your purpose.

Two commonly-used methods are:

■ sequential notes

■ nuclear notes.

Sequential notes

Sequential notes involve listing the key points under a series of headings and sub-headings. With this method you can:

■ number the points

■ emphasise material by underlining, using different colours or capital letters, though this slows some people down and so may not be appropriate for notes taken from lectures, television or radio programmes

■ use abbreviations, though be careful that you are consistent and can remember what the abbreviations mean.

Nuclear notes

Nuclear notes are more visual. With this method you:

■ write the main topic in the centre of the page

■ write related ideas around it and link them up to show their relationship to the main idea

■ add links around the edges to show relationships.

Activity

Both methods have their advantages. Try out both methods by making notes on Unit 3 of this course, on reading.

1   Make one set of sequential notes, making a list of the main points and including headings and sub-headings.

2   Make another set of nuclear notes, writing the word 'reading' in the middle of a blank sheet of paper and then writing the other points around this.

   Glance at my examples on the next two pages if you need a clearer idea of what the notes should look like.

3   Then note down which method you found most useful, and why.

Comment

Nuclear notes can be very useful if you want to generate ideas – perhaps for an essay or during brainstorming (see Unit 2, *Being creative*). They also have the advantage that you can show links between ideas which can help you to understand and remember them.

Sequential notes are useful when a topic is easily sub-divided under a number of headings, or when a book or talk is ordered in a way that is easy to follow.

You may find that one method suits you best. I use both in different circumstances.

Here are my example notes on Unit 3, *Reading*. Don't feel your notes must be identical – you are making them for a different purpose and you may want more or less detail, or to highlight other points.

Example 1: Sequential notes

How to Study Effectively

Richard Freeman and John Meed

pub. National Extension College, 1999, ISBN 1 85356 815 5

Unit 3: Reading (pp 37-50),

Reasons for reading:

- *obtaining a piece of information*
- *answering a question*
- *gaining detailed information*
- *trying to understand something*
- *pleasure.*

Ways of reading:

- *skimming – looking through a book quickly*
- *scanning – searching for a particular point – involves:*
  - *using references*
  - *flicking through the pages*
  - *using your experience*
- *reading to understand – detailed study*
- *word-by-word reading – rarely needed*
- *reading for pleasure – e.g. a novel*

SQ3R:

- *survey – like skimming*
- *question – ask questions before you read*
- *read – look for answers to your questions; form a judgement of the passage*
- *recall – check you can remember the main ideas*
- *review – was your memory right?*

Example 2: Nuclear notes

I found that when I made these notes I was able to jump around the unit more quickly. I also found quite a few links between parts of the unit.

```
How to Study Effectively                                       skimming
Richard Freeman and John Meed
Unit 3: Reading (pp. 37–50),              scanning


                                   How to read

                        ┌─── to understand
      Why read? ────────┤
                        │              word-by-word
  for info              └──────────────── for pleasure

          detailed          ⬭ reading ⬮

    specific
                                              Survey

    to answer questions ──────────────────── Question

                                           SQ3R      Read

  Reading quickly                                  Recall
                                              Review
    is it important?      should I do it?
```

How will you store your notes?

You will want to store your notes so that you do not lose them, and can find them again easily, perhaps for some coursework or for revision. So you will need to design a good filing system.

There are two aspects to a filing system:

■ what you use to store the notes in

■ how you classify the notes.

Ways of storing notes

This table compares some of the more common ways of storing notes.

Method	*Implications*
Loose-leaf folders	Easy to sub-divide and add to later.
Ring binder	Also easy to add to; sheets less likely to fall out. Material could be kept in plastic pockets.
Filing cards	Easy to shuffle and reorganise. Good for project, essay or report plans
Notebook	Convenient to carry. Pages cannot fall out.
Concertina file	Has ready-made sub-divisions.
Wordprocessor	Easy to edit material and to reuse for other writing. Remember to make back-up copies.
Tape recorder	Good if you find it easier to say things than write them down. Useful for recording speech too.

Ways of classifying notes

Within your filing system, you need to organise your notes so you can find them again.

Method	*Implications*
By date	May be useful for a series of lectures. You may forget when you made notes, though.
By first letter	A simple system to use. May let you down if you make a lot of notes.
By topic	Often the best system as it is easy to add to as you go along. But you need to choose topics that are easy to file under.
A mixture	For example, alphabetically within topics.

Activity

Think about the notes you will need to make. How will you store them? And what will be the best way of classifying them? Write your plans in the box below.

Comment

Whichever system you adopt, make sure that:

■ it is easy to decide where you will put new notes – if you can't decide where to put something, this may mean that your categories are not working

■ it is easy to find them later – consider using an index if this helps

■ it is easy to identify individual notes – they should all have clear headings.

This unit so far has focused on using notes to record information. We will complete the section by exploring two important sources of information: libraries and the Internet.

Using the library

Your public library may be one of your main sources of information, so it pays to make the most of it. You should become a member if you are not one already. Your library is likely to have both a lending section and a reference section.

The lending section

The lending section is usually the largest part of the library, and any of the books in it may be borrowed by members of the library. The books within this section generally fall into two main categories:

■ non-fiction

■ fiction.

Non-fiction

Nearly all public libraries use the Dewey Decimal System to arrange their non-fiction books. Under this system, books are arranged on the shelves in ten main categories:

000	General works	**500**	Pure science
100	Philosophy	**600**	Applied science
200	Religion	**700**	Arts and recreation
300	Social sciences	**800**	Literature
400	Linguistics	**900**	History

Each of these categories is then broken down into further sub-sections. To find a book you need to find its Dewey classification, and then look it up on the appropriate shelf.

Fiction

Fiction is usually shelved in alphabetical order, according to the author's surname and initials. So books by Richard Adams come before those by Kingsley Amis, and books by Kingsley Amis come before books by Martin Amis.

The reference section

Any member of the public may use the reference section of a library, whether or not he or she is a member. However, you must use these books in the library and you cannot borrow them. The reference section is likely to contain dictionaries, directories, atlases and so forth.

Other resources

Your library may also:

- lend records, CDs, cassettes or videotapes

- keep material on microfilm

- offer computer services such as Prestel.

Using the Internet

The Internet is becoming an increasingly valuable source of information, and if you have access to a computer and Internet connection – whether at home, work or college – it is worth learning how to make use of it.

The Internet may be useful to your study in several ways. For example:

- You may be able to find information directly via the Internet. For example, a student researching Californian earthquakes identified a number of eye witness accounts which had been recorded by the San Francisco fire service, together with descriptions of the earthquake and damage caused.

- You may be able to find references to other sources – such as books or journal articles – that you can then obtain via the library. Many journals have web sites listing the contents of their publications.

- You may be able to find details of organisations that you could contact for information.

- On some courses, students are encouraged to make electronic mail (e-mail) contact with each other to share ideas.

There are three basic ways of obtaining information on the Internet:

- If you have an Internet address for a particular site you can go straight to it.

- Alternatively, you can use a 'search engine' to search for information for you. Examples of search engines include Excite and Yahoo. They all work in similar ways – you simply type in one or more words and ask them to search for relevant sites.

- Most sites have links to other, similar sites. So once you find one relevant site, you can link up to other sources of information.

Don't expect miracles at first – you may not be lucky with your first search, and it is easy to waste time in the early stages. However, as you get more experienced you will find out more about which searches are likely to work – and when to give up if you're not getting anywhere!

To find out more about how to use the Internet there are several options.

■ If you have access to a college library, ask them to show you how to do a search.

■ If there is an Internet Café near to you, they are likely to run training sessions where you can find out how to use the net.

■ Otherwise, just ask a friend or colleague to show you how to use it.

Summary

■ Your purpose for taking notes will influence how you take them.

■ Notes must be easy to read, brief, clear, easy to understand, organised the way you learn and relevant to your needs.

■ There are particular points to bear in mind when taking notes from books or from speech.

■ Nuclear and sequential notes can both be useful.

■ Your method of storing notes should make it easy for you to file notes and to find them again later.

ACTION PLAN

Note below:

■ which methods you will try out for making notes

■ how you will store your notes

■ how you will classify your notes.

Methods to try out:

How you will store notes:

How you will classify notes:

UNIT FIVE

Writing

Introduction

Most learners need to write from time to time during their courses; and many will need to write extensively.

Writing, particularly in academic subjects, can be daunting. You may have to use particular formats – like essays, reports or memos. And you may have to adopt a more formal style than you use in everyday life for letters or notes. Many people find the idea of sitting down with a blank sheet of paper one of the most difficult aspects of studying.

However, there are skills and strategies you can learn which will help you to write more effectively. In particular, this unit will show you how to focus your writing, how to plan it, how to do it and how to check that it is good.

Objectives

This unit will help you to:

- list the kinds of writing you will have to do

- identify the purpose of your writing

- identify the audience for your writing

- collect the information you will need

- plan what you will write

- write clear paragraphs

- draft and edit what you write.

Key skill

Writing is one of the main elements of the key skill *Communication*.

The writing process

All writing involves a number of stages:

- identifying what kind of writing you must do (the task), and who it is for (the reader)
- deciding how to tackle it – this can involve choosing a topic or analysing a question
- collecting information you will need – this may involve doing research or reading
- preparing an outline for what you will write
- writing a first draft
- editing and redrafting to refine it
- giving a final check before handing or sending it to the reader.

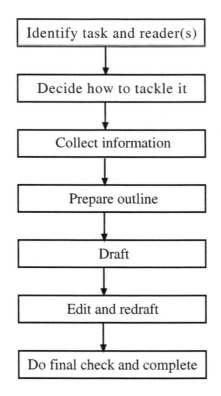

Identify task and reader(s)

↓

Decide how to tackle it

↓

Collect information

↓

Prepare outline

↓

Draft

↓

Edit and redraft

↓

Do final check and complete

Activity

As you work through the rest of this unit you may find it helpful to practise writing an essay of your choice. If possible, you should pass this to a tutor or friend for comment when you have completed the unit, together with the plans and drafts you prepare.

If you are working on another course at the same time as *How to Study Effectively*, you may like to choose a piece of written work you must do anyway. If not, choose one of these possible titles:

1   Do a short project about how people learn. Talk to at least three friends or members of your family and ask them what they find difficult and how they try to overcome these difficulties. Draw conclusions about what can help people learn.

2   Write an essay for this title: 'All tobacco advertising should be banned – discuss'.

3   Write an essay for this title: 'Mothers should always get custody of children after a divorce – discuss'.

4   Write a letter to your newspaper in response to one of the articles published in today's edition. Choose an article where the writer is arguing a particular point of view, not just stating facts.

What will you write?

Traditionally, most student writing involved essays. And you may well have to do some essays in your own learning. But it is also possible that you will do other kinds of writing. These could include:

■   letters or memos

■   reports – of experiments, tasks or visits

■   projects

■   assignments or coursework.

You will probably be writing for more than one person. Your notes may just be for your reading, or for other learners. An essay or assignment may be for your tutor or an examiner. A report might be for someone at work. It is very important to be clear about who the reader or readers will be – they may expect you to say certain things, and they will certainly expect to be able to read your writing!

In addition, some kinds of writing have particular requirements and conventions, so it is very important to be clear about exactly what you will be asked to do.

This activity asks you to think about what you may have to write in your learning. If you are not sure about what your writing may involve, ask your tutor for guidance. If necessary, just look through the activity, comment quickly now and come back to it later.

Activity

Look through the following list and tick those kinds of writing you may have to do in your learning.

❏ notes	❏ memos
❏ letters	❏ projects
❏ reports	❏ assignments
❏ essays	❏ summaries
❏ exams	❏ coursework
❏ projects	❏ other:

Then, note down each kind of writing you ticked and decide which person or people will read it.

Finally, note down special features of each kind of writing – for example, whether you should use certain headings, whether you should write in sentences and paragraphs or whether notes will be acceptable. Again, check with your tutor if necessary.

Type of writing	Who will read it?	Special features

Comment

You may need to ask yourself a number of key questions, such as those below.

❑ How long should it be? Many assignments, reports and essays specify lengths.

❑ Should you use headings? Essays do not usually use headings, while reports often use standard headings like Introduction, Method, Results and Conclusions.

❑ Should you include other people's ideas, from your reading? In much academic writing you will be expected to quote what other writers have said, and to illustrate different views. In some cases you may be asked to list the reading you carried out at the end.

❑ Should you include your own ideas? In many essays or reports you should finish up with your own conclusions or recommendations.

❑ Should you include evidence from your research? This would be necessary if you were writing up a scientific experiment or the results of a survey.

There may also be points of style and presentation to query.

❑ Should you write in paragraphs or in note form?

❑ Should you use an impersonal style (it could be argued that…) or a personal style (I feel that…)?

❑ Should you type or wordprocess, or would handwriting be acceptable?

❑ Should you write on one side or both sides?

❑ Should you use single or double spacing?

❑ Where should you put details like your name and the title?

You can check these points by looking at your syllabus or past papers, or by asking your tutor.

....

How will you tackle it?

You will probably have some choice over what to write. In some cases you will have a wide choice – for example, if you are doing some research. In other cases, as in an exam, you may have to choose between a few topics or questions. It makes sense to choose a topic which you know and understand well rather than something new and unfamiliar.

If you have no choice and find yourself committed to an unfamiliar topic, find out about it before you even begin to plan your writing. If you can't understand a topic before you write about it you will be unable to select material for inclusion or develop a logical argument around the material you select.

To help yourself analyse a question or topic it is a good idea to underline the key words. These can be described as the important words, the ones that give the essential information. They can:

■ tell you how to proceed

■ help you to collect material which is relevant.

The following activity illustrates this point.

Activity

Here are three topics for writing. Look at each one and underline what you think are the key words.

1   Essay: Discuss whether the Japanese should be allowed to kill dolphins in Japanese waters.

2   Report: Investigate recent returns from customers. List the main reasons for returns and make recommendations for reducing the rate of returns.

3   Project: Investigate child care provision for the under-5s in your area. Talk with parents you know and ask them how much this provision meets their needs. Write up what you find out.

Comment

The words I underlined are:

1   Essay: <u>Discuss</u> whether the <u>Japanese should be allowed</u> to <u>kill dolphins</u> in <u>Japanese waters</u>.

2   Report: <u>Investigate recent returns</u> from <u>customers</u>. <u>List</u> the main <u>reasons</u> for returns and <u>make recommendations</u> for <u>reducing</u> the <u>rate</u> of returns.

3   Project: <u>Investigate child care provision</u> for the <u>under-5s</u> in <u>your area</u>. Talk with <u>parents</u> you know and ask them <u>how much</u> this <u>provision</u> meets their <u>needs</u>. <u>Write up</u> what you find out.

Collecting information

Collecting information involves a number of possible tasks:

■   writing down what you already know on the subject

■   asking questions to which you hope to find answers in your reading or research (see also Unit 2, *Learning effectively*)

■   finding answers to the questions

■   recording what you find out.

Activity

Look again at this question:

'Discuss whether the Japanese should be allowed to kill dolphins in Japanese waters.'

Note down:

- what you already know about this
- what questions you would wish to answer
- where you might be able to find the answers to your questions.

What you know already:

Questions to answer:

Sources of information:

Comment

Known information might include:

- Dolphins are a protected species in most parts of the world.
- There is a strong lobby group in America and Europe whose aim is to protect dolphins.
- The Japanese fishermen are poor and kill the dolphins because they compete for the fish.

Questions to answer might include:

- Are dolphins an endangered species or are their numbers on the increase?
- How far do Japanese waters extend?
- Are there international rules about killing dolphins?
- Are there unusually high concentrations of dolphins in Japanese waters?

Possible sources of information to answer these questions include:

- your own notes

- your reading list or tutor's recommendations

- the Internet

- the library index – the subject catalogue for the topic should list any books on this topic; you could look up possible authors from your reading list in the author catalogue; and you could also look up the periodicals' indexes to find a recent article on this topic.

See Unit 4 for more on finding information in the library or on the Internet.

Use all available sources of information. Don't forget that there are sources other than books and periodicals (e.g. radio and television programmes). Discussions with others doing the same course may be useful too.

Recording information

If you are writing something long, like a project or an essay, you will need to record the information you collect. You will need to choose one of the note-taking methods described in Unit 4, *Keeping notes*. You may find it helpful to:

- use index cards to record useful quotations – on one side of the card you can write the quotation and on the other a reference to where it came from

- use separate sheets of paper to answer each of your questions, and record any relevant quotations or ideas on each one.

When you record a quotation from a book, make sure you include a full reference citing the chapter and page number together with the author, publisher and possibly the ISBN number.

Preparing a plan

A plan is a series of headings with an idea or two under each heading. The headings should do no more than cover the points you intend to write about.

The priority in the plan is logical order. This does not mean that there is one, and only one, order which you can consider but it does mean that your final order must justify itself and be clear to the reader.

One way of doing this is to look at the material you have collected and decide which are the main points you wish to cover. Your plan would then look like this:

- Introduction: define your terms and indicate how you intend to tackle the topic.

- Main sections.

- Summary or conclusion: recall the issues raised in the introduction, draw together the points you made in the main sections and explain the overall significance of your conclusions.

Activity

Look back at Unit 4, *Keeping notes*. Then write out a plan for this unit below.

Introduction:

Main sections:

Summary/conclusion:

Comment

My plan looks like this:

Introduction
Main points to cover
Objectives

Section 1: Why take notes?
Main reasons: to help remember something, to keep a record, to help planning, to re-order material, to help understanding, to aid concentration, to show other people
Activity – why you make notes

Section 2: How useful are your notes?
Notes should be easy to read, brief, clear, easily understood, organised the way you learn and relevant to your needs
Activity – analyse your notes

Section 3: Taking notes from written sources
Key points to bear in mind

Section 4: Taking notes from speech
Key points to bear in mind

Section 5: Different types of notes
Sequential and nuclear notes
Activity – try them out and compare them

Section 6: How will you store your notes?
Different methods: loose-leaf folders, ring binder, filing cards, notebook, concertina file, wordprocessor, tape recorder
Classifying notes: by date, first letter, topic
Activity – think through which method will suit you

Section 7: Using the library
The lending section: fiction and non-fiction – the Dewey Decimal System.
The reference section: directories etc.
Other resources: e.g. Internet access, etc.

Section 8: Using the Internet
Uses of Internet: information, references, contacts.
Access to the Internet: search engines, links.
Sources of help: library, internet café, friends.

Summary/conclusion
Key points/action plan

Length

A limitation on your outline is length. If you are set a limit of 2,000 words you will have to be far more selective than for 5,000 words. Make sure that you take this into account at the outline stage. If you don't you will have to replan in the middle of writing.

If you are given a limit of 2,000 words you might split it up like this:

■ Introduction   250 words or less

■ Main sections   1,200–1,400 words – say 150 per section

■ Summary/conclusion   500 words or so.

Activity

Plan what you will do for the essay you chose in the first activity in this unit.

Drafting

Once you have collected the information you need and prepared a plan, you are ready to start writing. Very few writers get it right first time, and most good writers begin with a first draft which they then revise. As I write this section, I am doing just that.

Advantages of drafting include:

■ you don't have to get it right first time, and this sometimes makes it easier to start writing

■ you don't have to start at the beginning – the introduction can be difficult to write, so it might make sense to start in the middle

■ you can change the order of things if they don't work in practice

■ you don't have to worry about getting your style and spelling correct at first – you can come back and correct them later.

If you have access to a wordprocessor, then drafting becomes easier – you can try out pieces of writing and then edit or reorder them without having to rewrite everything out again.

Key points during the drafting stage include paragraphing, using ideas and evidence, and using illustrations. We will explore these in more detail now.

Paragraphs

At the first draft stage you should aim to write one paragraph (or more) for each of the headings in your outline. We have already met some of the rules for good paragraphs in Unit 3, *Reading*:

- each paragraph should contain one main idea – from your outline

- the first sentence should, if possible, introduce this idea

- other sentences should support the main idea by explaining it more, giving examples or linking it to other paragraphs

- it is very dangerous to introduce a second idea as this will almost certainly confuse the reader.

Ideas and evidence

In most kinds of writing, you will wish to put forward your own and other people's ideas. Make sure that you:

- express ideas clearly and concisely

- back them up with evidence, whether from your own research or as quotations from your reading

- give credit where it's due – for example, if you quote from a book, give the title, author and publisher.

Illustrations

Also at the first draft stage, you should be thinking about whether, and how, you should illustrate what you write. Depending on what you are writing, you may wish to draw your own pictures – diagrams, charts, maps, graphs or tables – or to include copies of pictures from other sources.

Any illustrations should:

- be relevant to what you are saying

- be clear and simple to understand

- add usefully to what is already there

- be clearly labelled and, if from another source, fully referenced.

Getting started

It's often difficult to get started on writing. Here are some ideas:

- Remember it's only a first draft.

- Start with an easy part.

- Try a brainstorming exercise (see Unit 2, *Learning effectively*) to clear your mind and get you going.

- Rewrite your outline over two or three pages with headings and lots of white space, and then start filling in the gaps.

Activity

Prepare a first draft of your essay, drawing on the plan you have prepared.

Editing and redrafting

When your first draft is complete, edit and redraft it. Editing involves reading through and checking what you have written; redrafting means revising in the light of your editing comments.

Editing

As you read through what you have written, you can write your comments on the draft itself. Minor changes (say to spelling) you can correct on the spot. For more major problems you may wish to write the comment in the margin and think about how to improve it. You could ask someone else to help with the editing process. They may spot things that you miss, and tell you the things they like about it!

Activity

What kinds of things might you look for as you edit something you have written? Note down your thoughts below. If possible, look at something you have written recently to give you some ideas.

Comment

Below is a list of some of the things you might check are included.

Coverage

- Have you answered the question/followed the instructions?

- Have you included all the points from your plan?

- Is everything relevant to the question or topic?

- Is there anything you need to add?

- Is there anything you can delete?

- Is the order right?

Approach

- Have you backed up all your ideas with evidence?

- Is the balance between points right?

- Does the introduction give a clear idea of what is to come?

- Is the conclusion strong enough?

Style

- Is each paragraph limited to one main idea?

- Is it easy to read and understand?

- Could you say anything just as well in fewer words?

- Does the grammar, punctuation and spelling need correcting?

Redrafting

How you implement your changes in a redraft will depend on how you are working:

- if you have a wordprocessor or computer, you can make all your changes and then print it out again

- if you are writing or typing you will have to decide whether whole pages need rewriting, or whether you could make changes to the draft without it looking too messy.

Always bear in mind who will read it. If you are submitting a piece of work for someone you don't know (like an examiner), you will want to aim at a high quality of presentation. But if, say, it is a draft of a piece of coursework that you will revise in the light of your tutor's comments, all that really matters is that it is easy to read. And if the reader is just you – perhaps because you plan to edit it again – you can probably get away with murder!

Activity

Edit and redraft your piece of writing now. When you have finished, ask a tutor, or a friend, to read through it and comment. If you choose a friend, pick someone who you can trust to make constructive comments. Explain to them that you have written the essay as part of a project to develop your study skills.

Completing your writing

You have now done the hard work. You should have an edited and redrafted piece of writing which you feel conveys well what you wanted to say.

It is wise to check it one last time, making sure in particular that:

- spelling and punctuation are accurate

- presentation and appearance are good enough

- your name and any other essential information are included.

You can then send or give it to the reader. Bear in mind that you can always include a covering note, to explain what it is and to mention any points you would like the reader to comment on, if this is appropriate.

Extending your vocabulary

As you read and write more for your studies, you may find the need to extend your vocabulary. Textbooks often contain words that we do not use in everyday life, and the subject you study may well have its own specialist terms as well.

Extending your vocabulary is quite easy and is nothing like learning the lists of words which teachers used to be so fond of. The lists of difficult words printed in popular magazines do not, as claimed, improve your vocabulary. The mere learning of words and their meanings quickly fades from memory, and as fast as you take in new words you are losing words learnt two to three weeks ago. There are three keys to extending your vocabulary.

Read widely

Almost all the words you know were learnt in context. That is, as a child you heard others use the words over and over again in many different contexts, and so you learnt the meaning of the word. Any other method of learning would be impossibly complex for a child. Imagine trying to define 'pretty' to a five-year old! Yet most five-year olds use the word without the slightest difficulty. They do this because they have an intuitive understanding of what 'pretty' means from the various occasions on which it has been used by others.

Similarly, the best way in which adults can broaden their vocabulary is by reading widely so as to meet new words in a variety of contexts. It is, of course, no use just doing a lot of reading in one field. A diet of novels or biology or horror stories will not do. You would not meet enough new words in a sufficient range of contexts to establish them in your own vocabulary.

Use new words

Some new words will find their way into your vocabulary without any conscious effort. But you can also gain something by deliberately using new words as you meet them. It may help to list those words which you feel are of particular importance – for example, those which you will need for your studies. You can then look at the list and determine to use some of the words in the near future.

Look up words

On the whole, we learn very few words through consulting dictionaries. But occasionally you will meet a word without being able to grasp its meaning from the context. When this happens, look up the word in a dictionary and make a note of its meaning. You can go over such lists from time to time but don't try to commit them verbatim to memory. You may also find it useful to have a thesaurus to hand.

Summary

■ The writing process involves a number of stages.

■ Different types of writing may need to be tackled differently.

■ Always analyse the question, topics or instructions.

■ Collect the information you need.

■ Produce a plan before you start writing.

■ Writing involves drafting, editing and redrafting – you can afford to make mistakes first time provided you check it carefully.

ACTION PLAN

Note down any aspects of your writing that you will try to work on.

Assessment

Introduction

Assessment is the way in which your success at learning will be measured, and the way your achievement will be recognised.

Doing well in assessment is, again, a special skill. It's not just a matter of hoping that your skills and knowledge will come across automatically; you need to present them effectively. And this involves:

- being clear about how exactly you will be assessed

- planning your approach to assessment

- preparing effectively for your assessment.

This unit looks at these points in turn, and concludes with a section on how to tackle exams.

Objectives

This unit will help you to:

- find out how you will be assessed

- plan how to tackle your assessment

- plan your revision

- develop suitable exam strategies.

How will you be assessed?

Assessment has changed rapidly in recent years. Exams are no longer seen as the best way of testing much that is learnt. While they are still important, particularly on 'A' level courses, elsewhere other forms of assessment are often used, with or without exams.

Two methods of assessment have become particularly important.

■ Assessment of **coursework** covers what you do during your course, including projects, assignments and practical work. Coursework is widely used these days for GCSE, 'A' level and degree courses.

■ Assessment of **competence** covers what you do at work, the skills and abilities that you use every day. Competence is central to National Vocational Qualifications (NVQs) and General National Vocational Qualifications (GNVQs).

The first step in preparing for assessment is to be clear about exactly how you will be assessed and what the assessor expects of you. This activity will guide you through this process. If you do not know the answers to some of these questions now, arrange to talk it over with your tutor or to look at a copy of your course syllabus.

Activity

Look through the following list of types of assessment, and tick those which will apply to you. Then find out:

■ what you will be asked to do; for example, a choice of four essay questions out of 20, a paper of 50 compulsory multiple choice questions, or a project of 2,000 words with Introduction, Method and Conclusions, illustrated with diagrams or photographs

■ what the 'assessment criteria' for the course are – in other words, what you will be assessed on.

Assessment		Assessment	
Exam	❐	Assignment/essay	❐
Project	❐	Practical work	❐
Interview	❐	Competence	❐
Other:	❐	Other:	❐

Assessment	What you have to do	Assessment criteria

Comment

These are the assessment methods for four typical courses:

An 'A' level syllabus

Two exam papers, each three hours long and each contributing 50% of the total marks:

- Paper 1: Four essay questions out of a possible choice of 16 titles, each receiving 25 marks.

- Paper 2: Four questions: two compulsory questions (with a total of 50 marks) and two other questions out of a choice of seven, each receiving 25 marks.

The assessment criteria in the syllabus are very general, and described as assessment objectives; for example, 'to evaluate and interpret source material as historical evidence' or 'to present a clear, concise, logical and relevant argument'. I would want to ask my tutor for more details about how they are applied in practice.

A GCSE syllabus

Coursework (40% of the marks) and 2 two-hour exam papers (each 30% of the marks).

- Coursework: two to four short assignments of 1,250–2,000 words each, plus two or three longer assignments of 2,000–3,000 words each.

- Paper 1: 15 source-based questions, all of which must be answered.

- Paper 2: four questions from a choice of ten.

The assessment criteria are more detailed than in the 'A' level example.

A Certificate of Management Studies course

There are two main components:

- Using a learning contract and a personal development journal to record progress and evidence of competence.

- A project, based on two assignments, which can demonstrate the learner's knowledge and application.

Detailed assessment criteria are provided.

A General National Vocational Qualification in Manufacturing

A report exploring demand for a product, including explanations of:

- how consumer characteristics affect demand for a product

- how economic factors affect demand for a product

- the factors which determine product life cycles.

A forecast of demand for a given product presented in textual and graphic form.

Planning for assessment

Planning is important for all assessment. It is particularly so for exams – if you leave all your exam revision to the last minute you are unlikely to be able to do it well.

Ideally, you should plan for assessment as part of your overall plan for study. It is worth revising what you do from time to time in any case as this helps you to consolidate your learning. However, you are likely to need to start actively working on assessment six to eight weeks before the assessment takes place.

Activity

Draw up your assessment plan and timetable in the *Action plan* at the end of this unit.

- List all the pieces of assessment you must do in the left-hand column.

- Note down beside each one how you will prepare for it.

- In the next column note down the date when you will start preparing for each one.

- In the right-hand column, note down the date of the exam or the due date for the coursework, project or assignment.

Comment

As you approach the time to start preparing, make sure you:

- know exactly what you must do – check with the syllabus or your tutor; past papers are useful for exams, as well

- have all the resources you need – your notes plus any reading.

Preparing and revising

Revising is particularly associated with exams. However, you may need to revise for other types of assessment; and regular revision in any case will help you to refresh and deepen your learning.

One particularly important aspect of preparing for assessment is checking how you are doing against the assessment criteria for your course. You should have found out what your assessment criteria are in the first activity in this unit. There are three ways you can make use of them:

- if you know another learner who is tackling the same course, try marking a piece of each other's work against the criteria, and then talking about how you did it

- try assessing your own work against the criteria

- ask your tutor to use the criteria on a piece of your work, and to explain to you how he or she did this.

Make sure you try out one of these methods. If the assessment criteria are not clear or detailed for your course, ask your tutor to explain what he or she thinks really matters.

Other ways in which you can revise include:

- making notes from your notes – this will help you check that you understand everything, and will also help you to remember things

- preparing outline answers – it also helps to prepare other possible answers in outline form; this way you reorganise material and understand it better

- working with other people – if you can work with other learners, there is a lot of value in revising together; that way you can share topics out between you and check each other's work.

Activity

Note down here the revision techniques you might try.

Comment

Here is what other learners have suggested:

> *In the last term, five friends and I worked closely together. We divided up the course between us and each person prepared one topic and gave a seminar about it. I honestly feel I learnt more in this time than in the previous two years of this course, and we all did well in the exam.*

> *I worked out a timetable for my revision. I spread the topics I had to revise over the six weeks before the exams, so that I had so much to do each week. I allowed at least one free day each week to relax, and I made sure I stopped two days before each exam itself.*

Tackling exams

If you do have to tackle an exam, it pays to do so effectively. Use these checklists to help you.

The day before

Check, and tick off when you've done so:

❐ The place of the exam. (Be sure you know how to get there.)

❐ The starting time.

❐ Your candidate number.

❐ Your equipment:

    ❐ pens – including cartridges or a refill

    ❐ pencil

    ❐ rubber

    ❐ watch

    ❐ paper (if needed)

    ❐ calculator

    ❐ other equipment:

In the examination room

If you have a chance, choose an area where there is plenty of light and where you can see the clock clearly. Check your watch with the clock.

Tackling the paper

1   Check that it is the correct one (there may be other exams taking place in the room).

2   Fill in your personal details. Put your name, candidate number and any other details required on your first sheet, and on any other sheets as required.

3   Read the instructions carefully.

    ■ How many questions are you being asked to do?

    ■ Are any or all compulsory?

    ■ Do different sections or questions have to be on separate sheets?

    ■ Where must the answers be written?

4   Choose your questions.

    ■ Put a light pencil mark through those questions you can't possibly attempt.

    ■ Put a tick at the side of those you can definitely do.

    ■ Number the ticked questions from easiest to hardest. Do the easy ones first; this will give you confidence and allow more time for the more difficult questions later.

5 Check your questions. Re-read the questions you have ticked, and note the key words.

6 Make notes for each question. Points will flood into your memory in a random way. Switch from one question to another, jotting down the ideas that come to mind.

7 Ration your time.

■ If the questions have equal marks give them equal time.

■ Jot down a mini-timetable for your chosen questions, such as that below.

Quick notes on chosen questions	9.00–9.30
Q.1	9.30–10.00
Q.4	10.00–10.30
Q.6	10.30–11.00
Q.8	11.00–11.30
Final check	11.30–12.00

If you run short of time, do remember that you can't get more than full marks on a question (and rarely as much as that). So a good pass requires answers to as many questions as the examiners tell you to answer. For example, suppose there are 100 marks and you have to do five questions. If you do three well (say 14 out of 20 for each) you get 42 marks – not enough to pass if the pass mark is 50. But if you can get 4 out of 20 on each of two other questions, you would pass.

So, if you haven't done your full quota of questions and are short of time, use that time to write short notes on the remainder of your quota. In this way you should be able to show the examiner more of your knowledge than by a more elaborate answer to only one question.

8 Tackle each question in turn. Write clear, precise answers. Be careful not to over-answer. Each question should take no longer than the time allowed by the examiners but too often candidates take longer because they exceed the question. So, if a question is taking more than its fair share of time, re-read the question – you may not be answering it.

9 When you have finished the paper do the following.

■ Read through all your answers. Check for omissions, poor spelling and illegible phrases. Search your mind for any last minute points. (Better to do it at this stage, than to remember them after the exam is over.)

■ Check that your name is on each page.

■ Number each page and clip any loose sheets together.

After the exam

Do not waste time in 'post-mortems'. You have done all you can. Go out and relax.

Summary

- Find out exactly what form your assessment will take.

- Use your assessment criteria to mark your own work.

- Prepare a detailed assessment timetable.

- Plan your revision so that you don't leave it all to the last minute.

- Always read questions or instructions very carefully.

- Always plan your answers.

- In exams, make sure you have time to do all the questions.

ACTION PLAN

Draw up your assessment timetable below.

Assessment	Preparation required	Date to start preparing	Date of assessment

Further reading

If you want to read more on the topics we have covered, these books may be useful to you.

General study skills

Lewis, R. *How to manage your study time*, NEC, Cambridge, 1993

Marshall, L. and Rowland, F. *A guide to learning independently*, Open University Press, Buckingham, 1998

Rowntree, D. *Learn how to study*, Macdonald, London, 1998

Race, P. *How to win as a part-time student*, Kogan Page, 1992

Memory

Leach, R. *How to improve your memory*, NEC, Cambridge, 1994

Reading and dictionaries

Fairburn, G. and Winch, C. *Reading, writing and reasoning – a guide for students*, Open University Press, Buckingham, 1996

Chambers' English Dictionary, Chambers, London, 1998

Concise Oxford Dictionary, Oxford University Press, Oxford, 1995

Oxford Paperback Thesaurus, Oxford University Press, Oxford, 1994

Roget's Thesaurus, Penguin, London, 1995

Note-taking

Buzan, Tony *Use your head*, BBC Publications, London, 1995

Writing

Lewis, R. *How to write essays*, NEC, Cambridge, 1999

Lewis, R. and Inglis, J. *Report writing*, NEC, Cambridge, 1991

Assessment

Henderson, P. *How to succeed in exams and assessment*, NEC, Cambridge, 1993

Using the Internet

Holland, D. *The Internet for students*, Internet Handbooks, Plymouth, 1999

Signing off

We hope you found this course interesting and useful. Remember that to make the most out of it, and out of your studies, you must try and apply its principles at every opportunity. Developing good study habits is a slow job and requires perseverance. If this course has shown you what to do and it encourages you to go on and do it, it has achieved its aim.

Richard Freeman

John Meed